How to Bullet Proof Your LinkedIn Profile

10 Security Issues to Avoid

2017 Edition

Patrick X. Gallagher

Patrick X. Gallagher
As seen on CBS, FOX, NBC & ABC

v1

Table of Contents

Your Complimentary Report

As a way of saying thanks for your purchase, I am offering a complimentary security score-card spreadsheet to all of my readers.

In the Security Score Sheet, you will be able to quickly determine if a LinkedIn profile is fake.

In the content, I'm going to share with you how I score new profile connection requests using a simple Excel spreadsheet, which you can DOWNLOAD below.

http://eagertohelp.com/security

Foreword

As of September 2016, LinkedIn had 467 million users, making it the largest business oriented social network in the world. Tens of millions of those users log in and use LinkedIn every day, while tens of millions of users log on to LinkedIn rarely.

But the professional work records, passwords and in many cases credit card numbers associated with all of those accounts make LinkedIn a magnet for scammers, scrapers and phishing attempts. LinkedIn users need to know how to protect themselves and their personal information.

Patrick Gallagher has written a complete guide to protecting your LinkedIn data, and preventing opportunities for unwanted visitors to access your account. Creating and using a strong password is just the first of ten different ways to protect your account. This book is comprehensive, yet easy to follow for novice LinkedIn users, providing step by step instructions for securing your account against intruders.

Read this book and implement Patrick's suggestions. Your peace of mind is worth it.

  -Bruce Johnston

Introduction

As a teenager I dabbled in coding and hacked into a computerized system. It was a time management recording system used to manage employee time, and I created a dummy employee whom I called "Pinocchio."

By doing so, I wanted to show how easy it was at that time for security breaches to occur. My intention was to help the company take their security seriously and improve it. When their IT department discovered the breach, they quickly found me; I did not make that hard, anyway.

I explained to them how I cracked their weak security. After this, they offered me a job in their IT Security team. Back then I chose to turn the opportunity down. It didn't feel right. What they were offering me did not match the short and long-term value I would be building and sharing with the company.

Fast forward to today, and I have an even more security-conscious mind. You should as well. A security conscious mind really begins at home.

Whether it is protecting my online presence or improving the security of the back door of your property, it starts with good habits and principles you follow every day. By doing so, you will not only protect yourself, but your family too. You will be seen as a greater and more valued asset to the company you work for.

In a recent 2016 security compliance course I took at a client's headquarters. I scored 100% on the first attempt. How do you assess your security knowledge and best practices?

It starts with training and then implementing daily habits to protect your LinkedIn network.

LinkedIn has a very valuable database. That's one of many reasons why Microsoft purchased the company.

When a company stores as many online profiles as LinkedIn does, it becomes a perfect target for all sorts of hacking objectives.

In May 2016, it was revealed that LinkedIn had a major security breach. In fact, it turned out that LinkedIn had the security breach back in 2012. LinkedIn released a letter to its LinkedIn members, referred to as: **Protecting Our Members**. You can read it here: https://blog.linkedin.com/2016/05/18/protecting-our-members

What was leaked, or hacked? About 164 Million+* LinkedIn member accounts had their email and password hacked from the LinkedIn database. The passwords were not encrypted and are still available on the internet in plain text. LinkedIn said they invalidated all the account credentials for what was leaked. That's fine, but what if you used the same email address and password for other accounts?

A hacker could use that online information to check other social media accounts. Like the ones in the screenshot below.

Out of the 164 million LinkedIn members, probably at least 10% of them never changed their password, so those accounts can be used for whatever purpose the hackers intend. One way they can use this data: they can use the password leaks to add to their common password database.

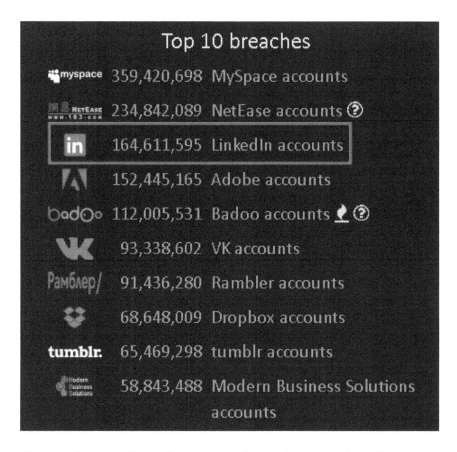

Top 10 breaches

myspace	359,420,698	MySpace accounts
NetEase www.163.com	234,842,089	NetEase accounts ⊘
in	164,611,595	LinkedIn accounts
Adobe	152,445,165	Adobe accounts
badOo	112,005,531	Badoo accounts 🕯 ⊘
VK	93,338,602	VK accounts
Рамблер/	91,436,280	Rambler accounts
Dropbox	68,648,009	Dropbox accounts
tumblr.	65,469,298	tumblr accounts
Modern Business Solutions	58,843,488	Modern Business Solutions accounts

Source: https://haveibeenpwned.com/ accessed in November, 2016

Then when they use a brute force password cracker, they have a new set of passwords they can use.

More and more people are using online accounts to access social media, their banks, and online ecommerce stores. What people do need to realize is that having the same password and possibly the same email for those accounts will help daisy-chain an implosion of a security breach.

In this eBook, I detail the Principles you can put in place to prevent your account being hacked through a variety of means—social engineering, database hacking, and key logging are just a few that can be leveraged to gain access to your account.

Think about it. Do you really want to give strangers access to your very important personal information? These days, if you keep your front or back door unlocked you would expect something to be stolen, right? How about making it easy for someone to steal your personal information from LinkedIn?

In this eBook, I will detail how you can even put a virtual padlock on your account by using secondary password protection. So even if a hacker found out what your email address is along with your password, they would not be able to login to your account because of the secondary virtual padlock you put in place.

Even if you only read the first Security Principal outlined in this eBook, you will be better off than most LinkedIn profile account protection put in place by LinkedIn members.

Note: The eBook, LinkedIn Security. Who's Watching You?: The Guide to Staying Safe from Personal and Professional Harm While Using LinkedIn, mentions that only "6.4 million users of LinkedIn had their usernames and passwords stolen and published on the internet."

Actually, it was a lot more than that, as I stated above.

This eBook will help you protect your personal information on LinkedIn.com. It might even lead to better security implementation for you on other online accounts.

*According to this site, https://haveibeenpwned.com/, LinkedIn had 164 million email addresses and passwords exposed.

As of today there are around 467 million accounts.
For more up-to-date information, refer to
https://press.linkedin.com/about-linkedin

Why I Wrote This eBook for YOU

"I am concerned for the security of our great nation; not so much because of any threat from without, but because of the insidious forces working from within." *-Douglas MacArthur*

Every day, every second there is a breach of security. Whether it's a company reporting the information or individuals—the effects of a data security loss are never entirely known. Most security breaches are made from the inside.

Reading this eBook will demonstrate how you can apply these security principles to lock your account down. You could probably apply some of these principles to other online accounts as well.

In this eBook you will get access to *10 Security Principles* that will help you "*bullet proof*" your LinkedIn profile.

With the LinkedIn data breach, you should realize that you cannot trust anyone to protect your data, 100% securely all the time.

The only person you can really trust is yourself.

Learn how you can protect your LinkedIn account and potentially use the same security principles for other online accounts.

If you got as far as here, "**looking inside**" this eBook and do not have an Amazon Kindle device, you can get a free Kindle Reader online that works on your personal computer. This will let you read this book and others instantly, click here.

Similar Keywords:1.hacking, 2.computer, 3.security, 4.testing, 5.penetration.

What You Will Learn

You will learn how the following LinkedIn options can be implemented. You can use this eBook as a guide, as you sit down in one sitting to improve the security integrity of your LinkedIn account.

- Who can see your connections?
- Important information about your public visibility
- Two step verification
- Opt into Secure Online Browsing for extra protection
- How to change your password
- What to look for in a Phishing email
- How to get your data archive
- How to avoid spending time recovering your data and securing your online account(s) because you did not follow these steps

I am determined to make your LinkedIn network more secure. I want to help you protect what matters most to you.

Reading and implementing these security principles will help you do just that.

Security Principle #1 -
Weak or Strong Password?

Treat your password like your toothbrush. Don't let anybody else use it, and get a new one every six months. *-Clifford Stoll*

Do you have a weak password?

What are some of the weak passwords that got leaked from LinkedIn.com? Here is a list of the top 5 that people used on LinkedIn.

#1 123456

#2 linkedin

#3 password

#4 123456789

#5 12345678

Source: https://www.leakedsource.com

Get yourself a strong password!

Have a strong password and only use it for your LinkedIn account. Don't use it for any other account. If you use the same password for the email account you have registered with LinkedIn.com, then a hacker can use that to gain access to your private email. Avoid creating a domino effect of security issues by having the same password and email address for all of your online accounts.

For suggestions on strong passwords, you can go here: http://lifehacker.com/four-methods-to-create-a-secure-password-youll-actually-1601854240

If you are concerned about losing your password, you can use an online safe like LastPass. I only use the online password vault to store passwords that are very difficult to remember.

To test your password and see if it is a strong password, check out this online tool – Test Your Password. The complete link is here: https://password.kaspersky.com/

What are some of the common passwords that get used on online accounts? If you go here, https://www.leakedsource.com/blog/linkedin it is obvious that some people only think of passwords as something easy to remember. The problem with that is they are typically passwords that have become automated in terms of using brute-force password hacks.

These are some common passwords that a LinkedIn Security employee talked about in their presentation on LinkedIn Security. Don't use any of these passwords, as they are all well known.

Once you have created and tested your strong password, here is how you change your password on LinkedIn.

Steps to change your LinkedIn password:

1) Hover over your LinkedIn photo (top right corner) and click on Privacy and Settings.

2) The Privacy and Settings section is divided into three sections: Account, Privacy, and Communications. Click on *Change Password.*

3) Enter your current password and then your new password. You will need to enter the password twice.

4) Remember to change your LinkedIn password every six months.

See the screenshot below for this information.

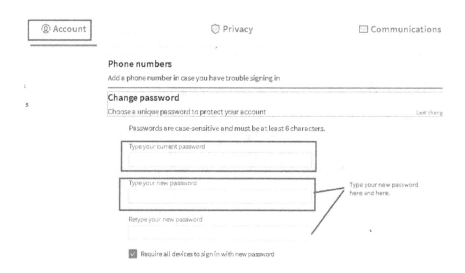

Note: Make sure you select the "Require all devices to sign in with new password." This way you will ensure your mobile devices will also use the new password to sign in.

Use one email address only for LinkedIn

This is so important. If you can keep your online accounts separate, it will prevent everything imploding if a hacker is able to gain access to your LinkedIn account, or if the information is leaked by a hacker, as it was in 2012.

I only use one email account for my LinkedIn social media account and a different one for my online bank account. You should do the same.

Get notified if your password is leaked

If you go to this site, you can be automatically notified that your LinkedIn account has been leaked to the internet. Click, or tap here for more information:

https://haveibeenpwned.com/NotifyMe

The only issue with doing that is that you will need to share the email address you have used for your LinkedIn account.

Quick link to your LinkedIn Profile settings:
https://www.linkedin.com/psettings/

Important Tip: To get the most out of this LinkedIn Security eBook, have this guide open on one device, as you go through the settings on LinkedIn.com on your desktop computer.

Summary of actions to complete

- Use a different email address for LinkedIn.com. Don't use your LinkedIn email address for any other online account.

- Choose a strong password. Use the Test Your Password utility to ensure you have a strong password.

- If your password is so strong you cannot remember it, use an online password vault tool, like LastPass.

- Don't use any of the passwords that were leaked, see the top 49 list, here:
  https://www.leakedsource.com/blog/linkedin

- Go to the next security principle.

Security Principle #2 –
Do the Two Step

"I get more spam than anyone I know." *-**Bill Gates***

Two step verification is like an extra line of defense. Think of ancient times back in the days of castles. They created two lines of defense. The first one was the moat. If the bridge was secure and protected by guards, the only way the attacker could get inside was go across the moat, where there were no guards.

If they managed to wade or swim across, then they would have to break down the door. Two step verification is similar. There are two steps to breaking through your security.

On online bank accounts, several banking institutions have implemented a security process that requires you to register the device you use to access your bank account.

For example, Chase will not let you login to your bank account if you try to access it from a computer that has not been registered. Their process requires you to verify who you are by sending you a verification code.

This code can be sent to:

1) A registered phone number. This is an automated call, where the voice calling your registered phone number will speak the verification code, which you must then enter to access your account, along with the password.

2) A mobile phone. The automated process will text you the verification number via SMS.

3) A personal email account.

Here is how you enable the two step verification method on LinkedIn:

1) Login to LinkedIn.com.

2) Click or tap on this link: https://www.linkedin.com/psettings/two-step-verification

3) Change by clicking Turn On. When you turn it on, the screen below will show the last four digits of your phone number.

Security

Two-step verification   Close

Activate this feature for enhanced account security   On

| Two-step verification is turned off.   Turn on |

We will send a verification code to your phone number ending in 9115.

Turning this feature on will sign you out anywhere you're currently signed in. We will then require you to enter a verification code the first time you sign with a new device or LinkedIn mobile application. Learn more

4) You will then be prompted to enter your LinkedIn password to confirm.

5) Then click on done.

6) Check your mobile phone for the verification number, then type it in.

Once complete, you now have that extra two step verification security enabled. If your mobile phone number is listed on your public profile, I recommend that you select a different telephone number for extra security.

To find out more about this important security feature, check out this link here: https://www.linkedin.com/help/linkedin/answer/544

Note: If you are using a landline as your registered phone number, you will need to change your number. Why? Typically your landline will not accept SMS text. LinkedIn will send you a text message using SMS format.

Summary of actions to complete

- Choose which phone number you want to register with LinkedIn it must be a mobile.

- Enable Two Step verification.

- Type in the verification number.

- Go and read the next security principle.

Security Principle #3 –

Personal Public Information

"The unlimited replication of information is generally a public good." -*George Dyson*

How much is your account worth? How much time did you put into creating your LinkedIn profile? In case you are not aware, many online accounts have a minimum price tag attached for a single account. For example, according to LogDog's research, a PayPal account is worth $80 as of August 2016. Here are some other examples of what online accounts are worth.

Examples of online account values

- Eharmony = $10

- Ebay = $10

- Amazon = $6

- Gmail = $1.20

For more information on what some online accounts are worth, read more online here: What your hacked account is worth on the Dark Web.

What information is personal to you?

Is it your name? Is it your date of birth? Is it your favorite color? Think about banks and government agencies for a moment. What information do they ask for when you access your account? It's typically your name and date of birth. Has much is your phone number worth?

Click or tap this link to find out all the vital personal information about you and what it could be worth.

Link:
http://archive.turbulence.org/Works/swipe/calculator.html

LinkedIn has this feature where you can enter personal information about you. Such as, what is your birthday, or what is your marital status? The birthday (month and day) information is not something you want to put on your LinkedIn profile. This can be used against you by a hacker. They can quickly build a profile on you with this personal information.

I can learn a lot about you in very few minutes. Even better if you have your anniversary date listed on your account that helps a would be hacker build out your online profile and confirm some other security attributes that they can use against you. **Don't publish your birthday details online, period!**

Your public LinkedIn url is listed under your profile photo.

Mine is: https://www.linkedin.com/in/mrpatrickgallagher

Here is how you turn off your LinkedIn profile from public view:

1) Login to LinkedIn.com (do this on a PC, or Mac).

2) Move your mouse over profile and click Edit Profile.

3) Right next to your LinkedIn profile public url is a "*gear*" click on that.

4) On the right hand side is: Customize Your Public Profile. Under that, click: Make my public profile visible to no one.

5) Then click save.

Note: If you want to keep your profile public but only turn off some items being presented to the internet (Google), or other search engines, you can turn them off in the same section above as well.

How to turn off your birthday:

1) Login to LinkedIn.com (do this on a PC or Mac).

2) Move your mouse over profile and click Edit Profile.

3) Hit the keys Ctrl+F and search for *"Additional Info"* – click on Personal Details.

4) Make your birthday blank for month and day. Clicking the *padlock icon* gives you options on who can see that info.

5) Once you have made the applicable update in step 4, click save.

LinkedIn even has a page on birthdays – https://www.linkedin.com/topic/birthdays

Summary of actions to complete

- Decide what you want to make public.

- Limit what you make public on the internet. Go into profile settings and review what you have made public.

- Don't display your birth date on your LinkedIn profile. Go into LinkedIn profile settings and turn it off now.

- Go read the next security principles and find out what more you can do to bullet proof your LinkedIn profile.

Security Principle #4 –
Gone Phishing for Emails

"The open web is full of spam, shady operators, and blatant falsehoods. Outside of a relatively small percentage of high quality sites, most of the web is chock full of popup ads and other interruptive come-ons. It's nearly impossible to find signal in that noise, and the web is in danger of being overrun by all that crap." -*John Battelle*

Gone Phishing for Emails

First of all, if you don't understand phishing, let me explain it very simply. Phishing is normally performed through email communications by a trusted source. The trusted source (which it is not) will attempt to get you to reveal some personal information about yourself, such as: usernames, passwords, and credit card details.

Also, this is backed up by a story by Stu Sjouwerman, who said you can warn other people in your network. In his online post he talks about the recent Yahoo security breach. Here is the story, *"These 500 Million Hacked Yahoo Accounts Are A Phishing Paradise."*

Again here is the complete link to the story:
https://blog.knowbe4.com/yahoo-500-million-hacked-accounts-are-phishing-paradise

Look for signs that the communication is not from LinkedIn

Here is what LinkedIn security said they do to ensure that the LinkedIn email is actually from LinkedIn.

- All valid LinkedIn messages come with a Security Footer (see screenshot below).

- LinkedIn will never ask you for personal information in an email.

- LinkedIn will never attach any files to their email communications.

Ask a question or share your ideas. Click here

You are receiving Groups Weekly Digest emails. Unsubscribe.
This email was intended for Patrick Gallagher (I help New Product Introduction Teams see the simplicity in the complexty | Internationally Recognized LinkedIn Author). Learn why we included this.
If you need assistance or have questions, please contact LinkedIn Customer Service.

© 2016 LinkedIn Corporation, 2029 Stierlin Court, Mountain View CA 94043. LinkedIn and the LinkedIn logo are registered trademarks of LinkedIn.

Example of a LinkedIn Email footer. This came from a LinkedIn group email discussion.

Look for signs that the email is not from LinkedIn.com

To do that, you can place your mouse cursor over the hyperlink. The real link will be revealed. If the link in the email does not direct you back to LinkedIn.com, then you know that this is potentially a phishing scam.

Leading indicators for phishing emails

The email will typically have some common English words misspelt, and the same goes for other languages. If in Spanish, the language used in the message will have bad spelling and bad grammar.

The message will communicate using fearful tactics. For example, if you don't do this now your account may get deleted. You must act immediately.

If you suspect that you've received a *"phishing"* email impersonating LinkedIn, please forward the entire email to safety@linkedin.com.

Summary of actions to complete

- Whenever you get an email from someone you do not know, do not open it.

- Do not click on any links within an email from an unknown source.

- Open your emails on LinkedIn.com; they will often protect you better than your internet service provider (ISP).

- Report any suspicious emails to LinkedIn.com here: phishing@linkedin.com or safety@linkedin.com.

Security Principle #5 –
Log In with Less

"The internet to me is kind of like a black hole, and I never really go on it." *-Jennifer Lawrence*

How many devices do you use?

These days there are so many ways you can login to a Web 2.0 platform. Mobility is getting more and more usage and with that comes multiple devices with which you can login. In my eBook: How to Amplify your LinkedIn Profile on your Mobile Device, I share survey results of how much mobile device usage has increased.

In fact, in late 2015, LinkedIn released a major user interface (UI) update to the mobile app.

With that new UI in late 2016, LinkedIn began to release a new desktop version based on the mobile app that they rolled out the year before. In 2017, you will see a major change that will impact the way you use LinkedIn.

My LinkedIn connection, Viveka von Rosen has already made some good comparisons about the UI changes.

You can read the details here: https://www.linkedin.com/pulse/what-difference-between-old-linkedin-user-interface-new-von-rosen

Summary of mobile devices

Mobile Devices (accessed via a mobile application) :

- Smart Phone
- Tablet
- Laptop*

*Laptop will use a browser and not an app.

Summary of PC devices (non-mobile)

These web 2.0 platforms are accessed via a traditional web browser:

- PC
- Apple
- Browser

Each time you login to the LinkedIn network there will be details recorded about your visit. Your IP address will be the primary detail. That detail will give the host an idea of what city you are logging in from.

My advice is login with the same devices (one to two max). Don't be tempted to login via multiple browsers or devices. Don't use public terminal access, like libraries, or any other public access point that could possibly be compromised.

Use one PC and one mobile device. The preferred scenario would be to only login with your desktop to access LinkedIn.com. Most member updates to profiles are made online via PC/Apple desktop computers.

Many people prefer to make updates to their profile with a bigger keyboard and screen. In addition there are several features you cannot update via the mobile app.

I recommend using the PC version of LinkedIn.com instead of the app because you give so much away about yourself when using a mobile app, especially in the LinkedIn mobile app.

In my eBook: Pimp Your Profile: How to Amplify your LinkedIn Profile on your Mobile Device, I list out all the personal information that the LinkedIn app can access. Often much of it is un-warranted.

What's interesting is that LinkedIn currently does not offer a mobile version of the data they capture from you. You can't make a request for a separate mobile data archive.

See the section on requesting your data archive in Security Principle 8.

Summary of actions to complete

- Only use one or two devices to log in to LinkedIn - desktop or mobile. Otherwise you will quickly build an opportunity for a hacker to exploit your logged in presence.

- Get familiar with the Where You're Signed In setting on LinkedIn.com: See Security Principle 7.

- Don't login to LinkedIn using public terminals, like in the library.

- Logout of LinkedIn when your are finished.

Security Principle #6 –
Choose: Quality Over Quantity

"The Internet has empowered us. It has empowered you, it has empowered me, and it has empowered some other guys as well." *-Patrick Chappatte*

Being well-connected

What is your goal on LinkedIn? To be connected with everyone regardless of their network security policy? Do you want to connect with people that connect with "LIONS" or people that don't check if a profile is fake or real?

Avoid a connection with anyone who, after accepting their connection, immediately sends you an email selling lead generating software or other quick sale items. Remove the connection fast.

You should look at making your connections viewable only by you.

If you have first level connections that you view that have this feature enabled, then when you view their connections, all you will see is the connections you share with them. Anyone who has not enabled this feature is giving a potential hacker access to building profiles about you and your network.

There are many LinkedIn profiles that do not have this feature enabled. This is something you should review before accepting connection requests on LinkedIn.com.

As far as I can tell, there isn't an automated way to review 1st level connections, which a hacker would try and do if they gained access to your network by connecting with you. This is good news.

However, a spammer, or anyone who wants to build profiles about your network, would have to go through each connection one-by-one.

Here is how you turn it off.

Steps to turn off sharing your 1st level connections:

1) Login into LinkedIn.com.

2) Click or tap this link: https://www.linkedin.com/settings/connection-visibility.

3) From the drop down menu, choose: **Only You.**

In most cases it will already be set to *Your Connections*.

Note: People will still be able to see connections who endorse you and connections they share with you.

Summary of actions to complete

- Whenever you get an email from someone you do not know do not open it

- Do not click on any links within an email from an unknown source

- Now go and review the next LinkedIn security principle

Security Principle #7 –
Where Have You Been?

"As the Internet of things advances, the very notion of a clear dividing line between reality and virtual reality becomes blurred, sometimes in creative ways." *-Geoff Mulgan*

Believe this. All online activity is tracked, period. If you do not understand or know this, then search your online search engine for "online activity." For Google it can be downloaded via https://myactivity.google.com/.

LinkedIn also tracks where you login, what type of device you login with, your ip address, and so forth. For some time LinkedIn has made it possible for their members to get access to that information. You can get to it by following the steps in this chapter.

Log out of LinkedIn when you are done with your social reviews

That includes your mobile device. Go to Privacy and Settings, then see where you're signed in to find out where you are logged in...You will be surprised to see the total number.

When you sign out of all sessions, LinkedIn's security process will sign you out of all of the sessions except your current session. You can go and see your logged in sessions immediately by clicking this link:
https://www.linkedin.com/settings/sessions.

When you click on that link you will see something like this:

You're currently signed in to **2** sessions.

Here's a list of all the places you're signed into LinkedIn right now. You can see details about each session, sign out of individual sessions, or sign out of everywhere at once. You can also sign out of apps you've authorized with LinkedIn from the third party apps setting.

Link:
https://www.linkedin.com/psettings/third-party-applications

The last part of the message is very important and I will show you how to change the third-party security settings later on in this eBook.

Here is a screenshot of where that menu item for your LinkedIn session(s) is:

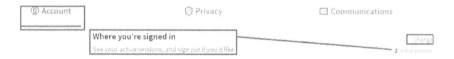

Again, you can get to the screen setting after you login by clicking or tapping here:
https://www.linkedin.com/psettings/sessions.

Steps to log out of LinkedIn:

1) Login to LinkedIn.com.

2) Take a shortcut to your settings by typing this in:
   https://www.linkedin.com/psettings/.

3) Under Account, then Basic,s there is a section titled:
   Where you're signed in. Click the word "*Change.*"

4) The section will expand and list your current location. Scroll down and click *"Sign out of all these sessions."*

5) Enter your current LinkedIn profile password, then click the End All Sessions.

The popup will disappear and if you had signed in multiple sessions, you should now see one session active. That should be your current session.

You will also notice that the browser type is listed. For example, **Chrome on Windows** might be one. There will also be a Town/City listed. When you click details, you will see the IP address and the owner of the ISP address.

Short link to the above profile settings location:
https://www.linkedin.com/psettings/account

LinkedIn checks your current IP address

If you travel a lot and work on different country IP addresses, LinkedIn will know that. For example, when I was finishing up an eBook in Poland I got this prompt before I could login to LinkedIn.com:

Linked [in] ®

Don't have an account? Join Now

Sign-In Verification

This login attempt seems suspicious.

Please enter the verification code sent to the email top-performe· to finish signing in.

Didn't get it? Resend to all emails

Submit

By using this plugin, you agree to the LinkedIn User Agreement and Privacy Policy

As a matter of security, you will need to have access to at least one of the emails you used to register with on LinkedIn.com. If you don't enter the verification code sent to your LinkedIn registered email account, you will not be able to login to the location your current device is being used at.

This is another great way LinkedIn helps to prevent unauthorized access to your LinkedIn account.

Quick link to LinkedIn profile settings:
https://www.linkedin.com/psettings/

Summary of actions to complete

- Check where you are logged in on LinkedIn.com.

- When you have completed your LinkedIn session, remember to logout.

- Now go on to the next section and learn about security principle 8.

Security Principle #8 –
Secure Your Privacy

"We become what we behold. We shape our tools and then our tools shape us." -*Marshall McLuhan*

Public Profile

In this section you should create a list of areas you do not want to be public. If someone is not connected to you, you do not want them to get your personal information.

In the section titled, Privacy, there are four sections: Profile Privacy, Blocking and Hiding, Data Privacy, and Advertising and Security. Get familiar with all of these sub-sections.

Here is a quick link you can tap, or click to get to the edit area: https://www.linkedin.com/public-profile/settings?trk=nprofile-public-profile-settings-redirect

When you select Edit your public profile, then the button titled "*Change*," it will switch to another screen (tab). To the right you can choose to turn off your public profile.

Your profile when made public is reported to search engines, like: Google, Yahoo!, and Bing etc.

You can learn more here: https://www.linkedin.com/help/linkedin/answer/41?trk=public-profile-settings&lang=en

Tip: You can also create a public profile badge in this section. See the link below.

Click this link to go straight to it:
https://www.linkedin.com/badges/profile/create?vanityname
=mrpatrickgallagher&trk=pprof-settings-badge

Suggesting your profile as a connection based on your email address

LinkedIn now has this option to share your connection information if they have your email address. You can change this under the privacy section. There are three settings.

Everyone on LinkedIn is the default setting.

Suggesting you as a connection based on your phone number

Here you can choose who can see you as a suggested connection if they have your phone number.

For my LinkedIn profile, I have chosen: Nobody. You have two other choices you can select as well. These are: Second Degree Connections, or Everyone on LinkedIn (default).

Sharing data with third parties

There are two settings here. I have chosen not to allow my contact information to be shared with third party applications and parties.

Choose Yes or No based on your desired outcomes for both options. I recommend selecting "No."

Advertising preferences

Choose whether LinkedIn can use cookies to personalize ads.

I selected, "No" here. I recommend you do the same.

Limit who can see your activity

The first place you want to become familiar with is the section under Privacy.

You can choose yes, or no in the Sharing Profile edits section under Privacy.

Typically LinkedIn trainers will recommend setting this to no, especially when you are looking for your next job.

Contact Information

Limit what you put in your contact area and who can see it. There are three areas you can put your contact information in on LinkedIn. Well, there is actually more than that. However, these three areas that I recommend should be looked at when you are looking at limiting your contact information, such as email address and phone number.

The first section is under your 500+ badge. It should say contact info. Remove your phone number from here if you don't need this information to be provided to first level connections.

Summary Section

If you are looking for a job and you want to temporarily have a recruiter gain access to a number they can call you on quickly I recommend you place the number here. Also in my eBook: Pimp Your Profile, I suggest you place the number in the first sentence. Otherwise you will not see the number.

If you want to be more secure on your profile, do not list your phone number here. Keep in mind that there are drawbacks to this strategy, such as making it harder for someone to be able to connect with you via phone, etc.

Advice for Contacting You Section

Further down on your profile you can list a number in the section titled Advice for Contacting You.

If you want to put your number here, this would be where you would also add it. To be more secure, you can remove your phone number from this section.

Browse Securely

Make sure your connection with LinkedIn.com via your browser is secure using https. In the older generation of LinkedIn, you had to turn this on. Now it is on by default.

Browse LinkedIn more securely with HTTPS, especially on public computers and in public hotspots with unsecured Wi-Fi connections. Just make sure your browser starts with https://linkedin.com....the rest of it □.

Like this example here:

https://www.linkedin.com/learning/meeting-the-challenge-of-digital-transformation.

Browse in Stealth mode

On certain occasions, for instance, when you are researching a client or a company and don't want your profile to come up under the section, **Who's Viewed Your Profile**.

For a different opinion on LinkedIn Security, view the Kaspersky Security tips here: https://blog.kaspersky.com/linkedin-security-tips/11757/

Summary of actions to complete

- Get familiar with the data privacy and advertising page on LinkedIn.

- Decide what people should see on your Profile.

- Decide what you want to make public.

- Implement the changes based on what you decide to take action on.

- Move on to the next section and learn about an important principle, security principle #9.

Security Principle #9 –
Data Sharing

"When we share our personal data with business, its use should be transparent and secure." -*Anna Eshoo*

For all of your LinkedIn activity, there is information about you captured and stored in a database. You want to ensure you know what is being captured. This information could be used against you without your knowledge. Or, if you are like me, you might be curious to know what information is being captured.

Why should you care about getting your data archive? Here is why. If your account ever gets deleted, or gets locked for some reason, you can re-create your profile using your data-archive. The amount of time you have spent on your profile will determine how important it is to get a copy of the data while you still can.

In 2017, about 100% of the LinkedIn population will be getting the new Desktop user interface (UI), so it's quite likely that some features will be gone and you won't be able to get access to that information once the UI is removed for that feature (where applicable).

Go get your data archive today!

Requesting your data archive

The first thing you should know about the data archive from LinkedIn is that it there is a lot of information stored in those archives. You will also not get the data archive within an hour, and it is split into two. You will get two emails within 24 hours with a link to the archive. The first archive link you will get within 12 hours.

You must click on that link to download the first part of your online LinkedIn data archive.

Click Request an Archive of Your Data to export an archive of your LinkedIn activity and data. It's a good idea to do this once a month so you always have access to your latest LinkedIn data in case anything happens with your account.

Here is the archive request link again:
https://www.linkedin.com/settings/data-export-page.

Here is a complete list of what is captured in your data archive:

1) Account status

2) Ads you've clicked

3) Ad targeting criteria

4) Causes you care about

5) Certifications

6) Comments

7) Contacts – those that you imported

8) Connections – 1st degree connections

9) Email addresses

10) Education

11) Endorsements

12) Group Comments and Group Likes

13) Group Posts

14) Honors

15) Inbox communication

16) Interests and Invitations

17) Languages and Likes

18) Mobile apps - mobile device LinkedIn applications that are registered with your account

19) Name information

20) Notes and Tags (vital as this feature will be removed by March 2017)

21) Organizations and Patents

22) Phone Numbers that you have associated with your account – IMPORTANT

23) Positions

24) Profile Information

25) Projects

26) Publications

27) Recommendations (Received and Given)

28) Registration – the date you first registered on LinkedIn.com

29) Search History

30) Security Challenges - Contains a list of all the challenge events for your account. This is vitally IMPORTANT

31) Shares – everything you shared or re-shared

32) Skills

Finally, there is a link you can use to request even more information captured about you that is not listed above.

You can also do that here by clicking on this link: LinkedIn's Data Consent form.

Once you request additional data and sign your consent, also known as, "LinkedIn and/or SlideShare Data Consent Form" a LinkedIn trouble ticket will be assigned to your account.

If you want to look at all of your LinkedIn cases, open or closed you can view them here: https://www.linkedin.com/help/linkedin/cases

Did you know that all this information was being captured on you? Follow the simple instructions below to get started on requesting your archive.

How to request your data archive

1) Login to LinkedIn.com.

2) Go here: https://www.linkedin.com/settings/data-export-page.

3) Enter your email address and password.

4) On the right hand side, click on Request Archive.

5) Click on the link you receive in the first email.

6) Click on the link you receive in the second email (24 hour wait).

After you have requested your data archive, the button in step 4 above will change to *Request Pending*. You can either go and check your email for the link to the first part, or wait for about an hour and refresh the data export page. If the first part of your data archive is ready the screen will change to a download button and will say, "The first installment of your data is ready."

If you would prefer to not wait and check your email within 24 hours, then look for this message below. The message will be titled: **The first installment of your LinkedIn data archive is ready!**

In 24 hours you will get an official LinkedIn email saying your complete data archive is ready. In minutes you will get your first email from LinkedIn security. This is what it says:

"Here's just the first part of the information we have archived for you, including things like your messages, connections, and imported contacts. You can download it with this link.

Within 24 hours, you'll get an email with a link where you can download the second part of your archive. It'll include your activity and account history, from who invited you to join to the last time you logged in. Want to see the full list of what's included? Just visit our Help Center."

Thanks,

The LinkedIn Team

Once you have downloaded the zip file you will need to go through all the information. You will need to enter your email and password again to download the zip file.

The first file will have a format of:
Initial_LinkedInDataExport_date.zip

The second file, message subject [**Your full LinkedIn data archive is ready!**] will have a similar zip format. If you don't download the second file within three days, the link in the email will not take you to the prepared file. The second file has a date format of:
Complete_LinkedInDataExport_date.zip.

Take a look at the second file you will be amazed what LinkedIn captures from your activity!

If you don't get your second file within 3 days of requesting you will get the following information.

Instead you will be presented with two choices.

1.) Fast File only or

2.) Fast File plus other data.

Recommendation: Don't forget to download your archive, both files, or you will have to request it again. You will request it again via this link: https://www.linkedin.com/settings/data-export-page.

Requesting a copy of your LinkedIn connections

If you want to backup your LinkedIn connections, you can request that as well. It will be a separate file. You can get that information much quicker than when you request your data archive.

Here is how you do it.

Steps to take to get your csv file:

1.) Login to LinkedIn.

2.) Click on My Network, then Connections.

3.) Scroll over to the right and click the gear icon.

4.) Then click on Export LinkedIn Connections.

5.) Click on Export.

6.) Type in text to match the *"Captcha"* text and click continue.

7.) Save the linkedin_connections_export_microsoft_outlook.csv file to your file folders.

That's it: you are complete. You do not need to do this if you have requested your data archive already. However, this process is much quicker and it's instant when you export your first level connection list (emails).

How LinkedIn uses your phone number

To prevent abuse - If we suspect potential abuse, we can ask you to provide your phone number as an additional verification to prove you're a real person. Learn more about security verification.

To help you reset your password - When you add a mobile phone number to your account, we'll automatically enable it for this purpose.

To help you find people you know - If someone uploads their address book and your phone number is included, we may suggest them as a connection.

Note: By March, 2017 you will no longer be able to get access to the notes, or tags from LinkedIn. That information will be available until March via the data archive request link. You can get that data and find it in the contacts file.

Click or tap this link for more information:
http://bit.ly/2h4YfkS.

This is a link to the help section of LinkedIn and the title of the help page is: Relationship Section of a LinkedIn Profile - No Longer Available.

Summary of actions to complete

- Request your data archive.

- Wait for the email, usually within 24 hours, then click on the link to retrieve your data archive.

- Review the data archive (1st and 2nd email) and check to see if there is anything unusual.

- Now go and read the principle #10. Protect your LinkedIn network by reading Security Principle #10.

Security Principle #10 -
Protecting Your LinkedIn Network

"There are two kinds of people in America today: those who have experienced a foreign cyber-attack and know it, and those who have experienced a foreign cyber-attack and don't know it." *-Frank Wolf*

Do you ever think of your LinkedIn network as an asset?

If you don't, some surely do. That's why they create fake LinkedIn profiles, to get the email addresses and other information of your high-value, authoritative network.

You engage on LinkedIn; connect with members and potential customers, participate in group discussions and publish your own content through LinkedIn's Publishing Platform.

All of this takes time.

Getting your high-value connections to **500+** is a meticulous process. So, while you use LinkedIn innocently, accepting most requests for connecting, fake LinkedIn members opportunistically lurk.

They want to connect — not because they want to do business with you — but because you are the window to a priceless pool of lead information.

You can identify fake LinkedIn profiles and make it a safer platform for you and your network.

How do You Spot a Fake LinkedIn Profile?

It's easy to spot fraudulent LinkedIn profiles that try to gain access to your network and then download the email addresses of your connections.

After a while of following this process you won't even have to follow all these steps, it will become an automatic process, one that protects your network and ensures LinkedIn remains a safe platform for the exchange of ideas and the discovery of talent.

6 Steps in Identifying a Fake Profile

1) When you get a LinkedIn Connection request from someone, always login to LinkedIn.com before clicking on the accept button in your inbox.

Why?

People with fake email connection requests might attempt to snag your login credentials by sending you a fake connection request. The connection request will take you to a fake webserver to capture your email and password. Yikes.

2) Once on LinkedIn.com, look at the profile and examine the photo (assuming there is one). If you are using Chrome you can install an extension called: TinEye Reverse Image Search.

This tool helps you find other versions of the same image. It will tell you quickly - if the name does not match the photo and/or profile. Here are two examples of fake profiles that tried to connect with me recently.

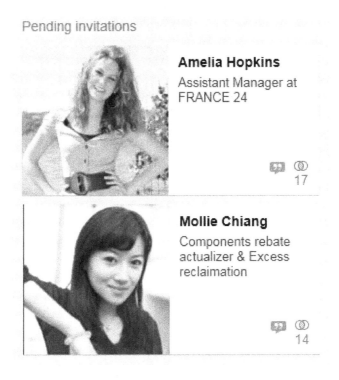

Why are these fake?

In the first photo, something did not quite add up. I instantly felt there was a conspicuous mismatch between the woman's name and her job location.

Let me explain.

Common sense tells me that if you work for a French company in France, it's highly likely that you're French too. In this case, the name is English not French.

I ran her image through TinEye and confirmed by hypothesis, that Amelia's profile is fake and that her attempt to connect with me was solely based on malicious intentions.

For Mollie's profile, my intuition instantly flagged this as a spammer. I didn't even have to run this picture through TinEye to know it's a stock photo.

Just to be 100% sure though I did go through the next steps in my fake LinkedIn profile identification process.

3) Click on the LinkedIn Member's profile name (not the "x" or "tick" mark). You should now be viewing the suspicious LinkedIn profile.

Scroll down to that person's Connections. On the top right of that box click on Shared. This will display all LinkedIn members you have in common.

You might think, "If others have connected with this person, then this wouldn't be a spammer, would it?"

Wrong. Some people want so badly to get 500+ connections they aren't as selective as to who they're connecting with. Don't be that person. Don't compromise your and your network's value.

Even if you share a few connections, don't accept their invitation just yet. (Unless some people in your network know or have talked to this person).

4) Check the Background Info - Typically, a spammer doesn't have a complete profile. More often than not, their education and current position do not make sense either.

In Mollie's case, she has given herself away, Hogwarts (sadly) only exists in Harry Potter. Gotcha! More often than not a fake profile is sparsely populated, there won't be much information filled in. Why? It takes too much time, which the owner of the fake profile isn't interested to spend on it.

5) Report the profile to LinkedIn.com - before you click on that "x" be responsible and report this fake LinkedIn profile to LinkedIn.com.

Here is how you do it - At the top of the spammer's profile click the Down arrow as seen below. Then click on "Block or Report."

Click on the Report box, then in the dropdown menu choose Flag Profile as Misrepresentation. In the details box you can be more specific: Fake LinkedIn Profile.

Click on the *Agree* button to report the profile to LinkedIn.com.

6) Close and Ignore. Now go back to your Add Connections Icon (represented by grey headshot with a + sign) and click the ignore sign.

You can go a step further and click the "I don't know this person (aka IDK). Note that this link disappears if you click away after clicking the "x."

If you prefer to skip all that you can simply click the "x" button.

LinkedIn: A safe, professional business network

When we ignore fake LinkedIn profiles we contribute to the turning of LinkedIn into a Fake Profile Heaven. Act responsibly, protect yourself and your network by consciously choosing who to connect with and who to ignore or report. Before I even finished writing this chapter, several more LinkedIn connection requests came in. All fake.

Please do your bit and report fake profiles to LinkedIn.com so that it becomes the digital hub of idea exchange and talent discovery it was destined to be.

Note: This activity needs to be executed from the web version of LinkedIn.com.

Fake Profile Links: "Amelia" and "Mollie"

Summary

In summary you have learned ten security principles you can implement in a short amount of time that will help your bullet proof your LinkedIn profile. In doing so you will make it more secure.

At the very least implement the recommendations and ideas discussed in Security Principle #1, #2 and #3.

Namely these are:

1) Use a strong password

2) Use a different email account for your LinkedIn account

3) Don't make your birthday public (month/day)

4) Keep your connection list private

Share on Twitter with your followers how you have read and implemented the security principles in this eBook. Click, or tap the icon below.

Banking Security

Depending on who you bank with you might get a bank that does a lot to ensure their client accounts are protected and they communicate steps you can take as a client. For that reason I have included below what I believe a good attempt to inform clients about internet banking security by a UK bank whose head office is in Hong Kong.

Your banking security is obviously really important to us. As technology evolves, the type of scams and tricks that people try to play become more sophisticated. Here's a bit more information on the type of scams that are out there - so that you can be aware, and know what to do if you spot something fishy.

Be alert for suspicious phone calls, texts and emails pretending to be from your bank, utility or telecoms companies - or even the police. At your bank we do everything we can to keep your money and information safe, but we need you to be wary as well. Fraudsters use the following tactics to obtain your information:

Vishing: Fraudsters contact you by phone, to try and get you to send your money to another account, or handing over cash/cards.

Phishing: Fraudsters send you an email, which looks like it's from your bank, to trick you into giving them personal and financial information.

* Smishing (SMS phishing): Fraudsters send you a text message, which looks like it is from your bank, to trick you into giving over your personal and financial information (by calling a number or clicking a link).

What you may not know is how to spot these scams and prevent yourself from falling victim, here are some tips on how to protect yourselves:

Be wary of unsolicited approaches by phone, especially if asked to provide any of your personal information, usernames, passwords or bank details.

[Your Bank] will never contact you to request codes from your Secure Key, ask you to generate a code, ask for your PIN number or ask you to withdraw/transfer money for fraud prevention reasons.

If you are suspicious about a call, don't be afraid to terminate the call and call us back on a [telephone number] - use a different phone line where possible.

If an email looks suspicious, do not click on links or download documents. Remember that whenever your bank sends you an email, we always include the last 3 digits of your postcode in the footer. If you see this, you'll know it's definitely from us.

If you have suspicions regarding a text message from the bank, call us on a known number to verify it was from us before acting on it.

If you suspect an email or text is Phishing or Smishing please forward it to phishing@bank name dot com so we can investigate it.

For more information on the ways that we keep you and your banking safe, visit the security section of our website.

We hope you found this message of interest. However, if you'd rather not receive future electronic messages about bank name products and services within Internet Banking, please select 'secure messages', 'compose new', then select 'marketing preferences'.

About the Author

Patrick Gallagher provides his talent & services to a major Fortune 50 company.

Patrick can be reached via his Admin at **(424)-703-GOAL**, or Click on his LinkedIn Profile.

For LinkedIn Coaching details, click here: http://careerconfidential.com/coaches-listing-page/

You can also connect with him on his Twitter page.

As seen on ABC, CBS, NBC & FOX.

SOURCES -Further Reading - Books for Reference

I put this list together based on current sales of similar eBook titles. These are the eBooks that Amazon is telling me that are currently selling very well. The top 10! Keep in mind that with the "**Internet of Things,**" this top 10 list may have changed by the time you get to this section and read this handy guide!

1.) Tor and The Dark Net: Remain Anonymous Online and Evade NSA Spying (Tor, Dark Net, Anonymous Online, NSA Spying), **James Smith**

2.) Complete Guide to Internet Privacy, Anonymity & Security, **Matthew Bailey**

3.) Cyber Fraud: The Web of Lies: US MARINE RISKS LIFE IN PRISON TO EXPOSE A CYBERCRIME THAT CONSUMERS KNOW NOTHING ABOUT,**Bryan Seely**

4.) Internet Security: Online Protection From Computer Hacking (Computer Security, Internet Hacker, Online Security, Privacy And Security), **James Cloud**

5.) LinkedIn Security. Who's Watching You?: The Guide to Staying Safe from Personal and Professional Harm While Using LinkedIn,**Greg Schroeder**

6.) Cybersecurity and Cyberwar: What Everyone Needs to Know, **P.W. Singer**

7.) Cyber Security Principles, **Garrett Gee**

8.) Social Media Security: Leveraging Social Networking While Mitigating Risk, **Michael Cross**

9.) Securing the Clicks Network Security in the Age of Social Media, **Gary Bahadur**

10.) Social Media Marketing Workbook: 2017 Edition - How to Use Social Media for Business, **Jason McDonald**

Recommended Websites
for Further Review

Web: **White Listing Applications,**
http://www.howtogeek.com/195381/ensure-a-windows-pc-
never-gets-malware-by-whitelisting-applications/

Web: **Anti-Virus Software that includes Whitelisting**,
http://usa.kaspersky.com/downloads/free-home-trials/anti-
virus

Web: **How to spot a fake LinkedIn profile in 3
steps**,https://www.linkedin.com/pulse/how-spot-fake-
linkedin-profile-3-steps-phoebe-e-waters-ma

Web: **VeraCrypt is a free disk encryption software
brought to you by
IDRIX**,https://veracrypt.codeplex.com/wikipage?title=Down
loads

Web: **How to Make Sure Your LinkedIn Account Is
Secure**, http://www.socialmediaexaminer.com/how-to-
make-sure-your-linkedin-account-is-secure/

Web: **How to change your LinkedIn Password**,
https://www.linkedin.com/help/linkedin/answer/2873/chang
ing-your-password?lang=en

Web: **Removing Old Saved Passwords from Your
Browser,**https://www.linkedin.com/help/linkedin/answer/5
354

Web: **Scary features of web
applications,**https://lnkd.in/by8bDXe

Web: **LinkedIn Chief Security Officer**, Corey Scott

Web: **Michigan State University Data Breach, 400,000 Records Exposed**, http://bit.ly/2f1H0BA

Web: **Here's how we help protect our members and customers**, https://security.linkedin.com/

Web: **Stay Safe Online**, https://staysafeonline.org/

Web: **What your hacked account is worth on the Dark web,** https://nakedsecurity.sophos.com/2016/08/09/what-your-hacked-account-is-worth-on-the-dark-web/

Web: **5 Ways to Protect Your LinkedIn Account**, https://blog.linkedin.com/2014/01/28/data-privacy-day-5-ways-to-protect-your-linkedin-account

Web: **Video: LinkedIn's Security Breach**, https://www.linkedin.com/pulse/video-linkedins-security-breach-viveka-von-rosen

Web: **As Scope of 2012 Breach Expands, LinkedIn to Again Reset Passwords for Some Users**, http://bit.ly/2ghnte8

Web: **How to stay secure on LinkedIn**, https://blog.kaspersky.com/linkedin-security-tips/11757/

Web: **Configuring LinkedIn for a More Secure Professional Networking Experience**, http://www.cid.army.mil/assets/docs/2can/CCPFLinkedIn.pdf

Web: https://www.linkedin.com/pulse/how-spot-fake-linkedin-profile-3-steps-phoebe-e-waters-ma

Web: https://business.linkedin.com/talent-solutions/blog/linkedin-best-practices/2016/7-linkedin-profile-summaries-that-we-love-and-how-to-boost-your-own

Web: **Yahoo one billion accounts hacked**, http://www.presstv.ir/Detail/2016/12/15/497968/US-Yahoo-hack-Verizon

Web: Find the source of your leak, https://www.leakedsource.com/

Other Books by the Author

Pimp Your Profile: How to Amplify your LinkedIn Profile on your Mobile Device
http://myBook.to/pyp

LinkedIn Secrets Revealed: 10 Secrets to Unlocking Your Complete Profile on LinkedIn.com
http://mybook.to/LinkedInSecrets

Write Your Book Outline: How to Create Your book Outline in 30 Minutes
http://myBook.to/outline

Publishing a Book on Amazon: 7 Steps to Publishing your #1 Book on Amazon Kindle in Minutes!
http://amzn.to/18i9JI3

Build Your Own Living Revocable Trust: A Pocket Guide to Creating a Living Revocable Trust
http://amzn.to/1OxVoM6

Spirituality in the Workplace: A Study Guide for Business Leaders
http://amzn.to/1NHROA5

Amazon Secrets Revealed: How to Sell More Books on Amazon.com
http://amzn.to/1Np2VaI
Email Inbox Management: How to Master Your Inbox with Etiquette
http://amzn.to/1JeKK8T

Love or Hate Email... 21 Rules to Change Your - I Must Check my Email Habit. Get Back to Work and Make Money Again!
http://bit.ly/Love_Email

Trapped in a Meritocracy: Cracking the Meritocracy Code: Get Paid More for Valued Performance
http://amzn.to/1zbufrW

Note: All these links are to Amazon.com eBooks. In most cases, the sales region is automatically detected.

Questions or Comments?

Congratulations for getting this far and reading this book! Now that you have read the book and put it to good use, I would love to hear from you.

You can send me an email to: LinkedInSecretsRevealed@gmail.com I read and reply to all of my emails!

Now please share your opinion and write a review

One last thing, if you believe this book has helped you and is worth sharing with other potential Amazon Kindle readers; please leave a review by **clicking on the button** below. Your review feedback will make the next version even better for future readers.

Create your own review

http://amzn.to/2hp9jKx

On Amazon, all 4-5 star reviews are like gold! I would really appreciate you leaving a 4, or 5 star review - it should take only a few seconds of your time.

The button above is for the USA. Here are the links for the UK, Canada, Germany and all the rest.

UK: http://amzn.to/2hilWGV
Australia: http://amzn.to/2gHzN97
Canada: http://amzn.to/2hiozIR
Germany: http://amzn.to/2gHxfbb
France: http://amzn.to/2gW9aL6
Spain: http://amzn.to/2gDDk9W

When you leave a 5 star review I feel like you have given me a gold bar like below!!

Thank You for reading and finishing this eBook!

www.ingramcontent.com/pod-product-compliance
Lightning Source LLC
Chambersburg PA
CBHW061020050326
40689CB00012B/2694